TO

AFAF, BASIL

AND LANA

WHO ONE DAY

WILL SING THEIR OWN SONGS

TO A LISTENING WORLD

The Songbird

A SELECTION OF VERSE

by
Helen Kinnier Wilson

SHEPHEARD-WALWYN

First Published in Great Britain 2000
by Shepheard-Walwyn, 26 Charing Cross Road, London WC2H 0DH

ISBN 0 85683 190 5

Designed and produced by Geoff Green Book Design

Printed in Great Britain by
St Edmundsbury Press Limited, Bury St Edmunds, Suffolk

ACKNOWLEDGEMENTS

I N PRESENTING the kind reader with a further slim volume of poems, I am conscious of the debt that I once again owe to all those who have supported it. I acknowledge, in particular, the help of Riad Nourallah, whose counsel and comment have served the manuscript at many points and who has prodded the work forward with an insistent loyalty. To my husband, James, I am grateful for his patient editorial work on the manuscript, in some part made necessary for a reason that may be understood from the last line of 'Beauty by candlelight'. And I thank also, although I did not know him, my late father-in-law, Dr S. A. Kinnier Wilson, for the drawing which appears on the cover, and which so well interprets the title chosen for the book. The several smaller illustrations which adorn the book, as in some part modified for the present purpose, are from his hand also.

It may be mentioned that the second poem of the collection, together with three others published in *Cambridge Reflections*, have been translated into Arabic by Dr Nourallah in an anthology of verse entitled *Nār wardat ash-shamāl*, 'The Fire of the Northern Rose' (Beirut, 1992).

C.H.K.W.

CONTENTS

PART I

LIFE LINES

THE SONGBIRD

"What shall I sing?" said the Songbird. "Shall I sing of morning and quiet skies, of woodland and country lanes and the turned earth?"

And the Wind answered the Songbird:

"Sing, if you will, of beauty, for beauty has healing hands. But the greatest of themes is life, as it is also the great mystery. Oh, sing of life, and the rich experience of life; nay, such are the heights and depths of life, such its patterns of light and shade, that never will you tell the sum of it or end your song."

And the Songbird answered the Wind, saying:

"Then of life shall I sing, of its hopes and high vision, of its challenge and adventure. Yet have I seen the wounds of life, and would hold in remembrance all who strive in loneliness through dark hours."

And the Wind spoke to the Songbird, saying:

"So let it be, O Songbird. And know that I, too, have a song which I sing softly through the trees when the sun is low. I sing that life is not lived alone, – that in its pleasures and achievements, as in its failures and in its sorrows, shine eternal things."

THE LOVE SPIRIT

My heart I will hide in an apple tree,
    And rest in the fruit of its bough;
And I'll colour your cheeks with sweet warmth,
    my love,
  And touch your red lips with the dew.

My hopes will fly high as the thistledown,
    The breezes dispelling my care;
And my song I will give to the birds,
    my love,
  They will tell you that I am near.

WHEN YOU ARE GONE

When you are gone the nightingale will sing
    a lesser song;
The path we oft have travelled, you and I,
Will seem, without you, empty as the sky,
    and ever long.

I shall keep faith with all you think to do
    while you are gone;
The goals you seek, the dreams you dream, I share;
Your sweet success will be my every prayer
    till all is won.

I shall be brave, and with my memories
    will journey on;
My task is now to teach my aching heart
To bear the pain that loved ones bear – apart,
    till you return.

THE KITE

I fly my kite on the windy heath;
    it is leaping and looping,
      swooping through the air,
And I all alone with the wind in my hair,
    heedless of care,
      on the windy heath.

High flies the kite o'er the slopes beneath,
    quivering, shivering,
      shimmering in the air,
And with it I run to I know not where,
    defying despair,
      on the slopes beneath.

I am a kite on the world's wide heath,
    swirling and twirling,
      whirling in the air,
Held by a string to a love that I bear,
    and a life that we share,
      on the world's wide heath.

SILVER LININGS

The goal is hard to see, the journey long,
And Earth bears ill the weight of human wrong;
    But soon the buds of May will lift the heart
And summer larks will trill the air with song.

The day breaks and the wheels of work engage;
The book of life is turned, – another page.
    But know, beyond the weariness of day,
The constant stars shine brightly, age through age.

At times it seems the struggle has no end.
But life has compensations, and may send
    from his great heart a gift as sweet as rare:
The loyalty and love of one dear friend.

BEAUTY BY CANDLELIGHT

Beauty is the light of the morning,
The call and resolve of the noonday.

In the play of children is she seen,
In the fine, straight characters of noble lives.

Hers is the authority of the poplar trees,
The dark secrets of the pine forests
    on purple hills.

She is the cry of the waves, the wings
Of the circling gulls as they turn unsteadily
    upon the wind,
The clouds in their high assemblies.

Such images I see again as dreams
Since evening fell too soon upon my sight.

I'LL NOT FORGET YOU

Though fortune smile, though times be stern or lean,
    If stand our souls together or apart;
Let our wings touch or heavens fly between,
    Within the closet secrets of my heart
        I'll not forget you.

Down the long aisles of sacred memory,
    Into life's forward path and winding lanes,
Where'er your footsteps turn – beyond the sea,
    To cities of the sun or distant plains,
        I'll not forget you.

While still my clouded eyes may greet the dawn
    Of autumn days; while softly treads the hour
And time is kind; while yet, o'er sand and stone,
    The advancing tide moves slowly to the shore,
        I'll not forget you.

THE OLD TREE

In the gardens where I live there grows
    an old and graceful tree.
She's a lady, tall and elegant,
    and very dear to me.
She has watched the seasons turning –
    but by age is not restrained
When, upon his invitation,
    she goes dancing with the wind.

A gingko is that tree, from lands
    beyond the rising sun.
In spring her leaves are lightest green,
    her trunk is darkest brown.
They fall, the leaves, with winter frosts
    together to the ground,
And like a golden necklace
    ring the mourning tree around.

A Persian poet called the trees
    'The tongueless ones': but, oh!
How much I'd love to talk to her
    and of her wisdom know.
I love her perfect manners
    and her quiet dignity;
I shall ever sing the praises
    of that old and graceful tree.

THE LANGUAGE LESSON

O polyglot, know quite a lot
    of words need careful screening;
From place to place – watch now this space! –
    they often change their meaning.

In gay Paris, you will agree,
    'Oh, formidable!' means 'super!'
But, s'il vous plaît, no more I'll say,
    pretence would not be proper.

To Rome we go, where, you may know,
    your 'jam' is 'marmellata';
I'll leave it there: the rest, I fear,
    would end up as errata!

To Washington we journey on
    where 'cookie' means a 'biscuit';
One could try more, – but OK, sure!
    much better not to risk it.

HIGHER WATER

With apologies to Henry Longfellow

Should you ask me, whence these stories?
Whence these tales and dissertations?
I should answer, I should tell you,
They were done in Cambridge city,
In, or close to, Cambridge city.
But when summer climbs the heavens
I have loved to travel northwards,
Passing through the open fenland,
Through the ancient Isle of Ely,
Through the town of Downham Market,
To the beach of Old Hunstanton.
There beside the laughing water,
By the shining Big-Sea-Water,
One may look across to nowhere
And find all the inspiration
That one needs for writing stories,
Lively tales and dissertations.

In such all-fulfilling moments
I have walked along the cliff-top,
Walked across the grassy headland,
Looking out into the distance,
Looking out beyond the sand dunes,
O'er the shining Big-Sea-Water.

PUNTING DAYS

Consider, now, the punt, –
a kindly and restful craft,
flat-bottom'd, blunt
at the ends and much the same fore and aft.
There is no mast,
sails have no part of it,
for it moves, but not fast,
by the thrusts on a pole
of a brawny operator.
On the whole
all learn the art of it,
sooner or later.

But pity poor Tom. One day
he was out of luck,
and got stuck
in the mud. So, there he was, clinging
to the pole like a koala bear,
while from all around,
as the punt slipped away,
the devilish sound
of laughter came ringing
in his ear.

W W W

They are wonderful things, these computers!
    When you're really on form and 'on line'
You can speed to the ends of the planet –
    Or alight at Newcastle-on-Tyne.

They will answer you back, these computers,
    For they're clever, you know, by and large;
They will say to you, 'Wait!' or, 'An error!',
    Just to show you who's really in charge.

Though, myself, I don't have a computer,
    For the PCs of others I care;
I am non-user friendly towards them,
    I am 'soft' on all breeds of hardware.

So continue, my friends, with computers,
    And your lessons think never to shirk;
Let the 'w's often remind you,
    They are 'wonderful things when they work!'

PANTOMIME

The curtain rises on a secret world
Which none may enter save the young in heart.
At once, from forth the pageantry of time,
The masked and spangled Harlequin appears, –
A saucy, merry-Andrew of a man
Courting the fair and stately Columbine.
The scene is now a bustling market town,
With pretty maids and breech-clad farmers' men
Dancing to pipes and bells in maypole days.
There quickens soon the pulse-beat of the play
As poverty and riches are enjoined
And work in concert, if at times opposed,
Toward the final good. From humble homes
Poor Cinderella, poor Dick Whittington,
Must in the end find favour's just reward,
And with the help of fairies on their path
Enter the gates of palaces. So, too,
Where eastern turrets claim the rising sun,
The golden magic of a genie's lamp
Brings fame and fortune to a widow's son
And purpose to a life erstwhile perverse.

With all the colours, lights and spectacle
The essence of the play is fairness. Wrong
Will always in the end yield place to right,
Magicians, giants, topple from their thrones,
As youth and courage meet the threatening day.
Oh, that the young in heart from every clime
Might know the joy – the spell – of Pantomime!

BIODIVERSITY

A poem written especially for Third Forms

God filled the world with animals,
    how many, goodness knows,
With lions, camels, antelopes,
    with bulls and buffaloes, –
The stately whale that through the gale
    serenely, safely goes.

The elephant He gave command:
    "Be gentle yet be strong!"
The loyal horse He like enjoined:
    "Speed man and maid along!"
The singing bird His order heard:
    "Go, fill the Earth with song!"

Bright butterflies of varied size
    and colour did He make,
And creatures that forsake the day
    and in the evening wake.
Such forms and shapes, – the friendly apes,
    the octopus, and snake!

PART TWO

LITTLE PHILOSOPHIES
AND REFLECTIONS

ETHNIC CLEANSING

Wild is my heart, tight though I hold the rein.
Determined, ruthless, pawns in Satan's game,
His men hold all to ransom, crying, "Mine!
Begone, who are not of our kind or race!"
Such foolishness calls for our pity. Shame
Will fill their final hours, and bowed disgrace,
When judgment shall her truth and power define.

And from this scourge the Earth shall have release
What time the wolf shall lie down with the lamb,
The leopard with the kid. Then will there cease
The chilling scream of war, and in its tomb
The very thought of war will man disclaim.
No longer shall the sword its place assume,
And nation unto nation will speak peace.

UNIVERSITY

To live and work in this most single place
Of builded stone and cloister'd histories;
To seek and search for truth in its vast store
And climb again the nine, long-suffering steps
Of that great House of Books whose humble door
Was e'er too small for its huge dignity;
To be a part of one collective will,
Of one great architectonic of thought,
That ever must explore and understand,
Advancing often by uncharted ways
Into new worlds, – such is the privilege
Of all who would the common vision share,
Of all who hold the call of learning dear.

THE ORIENTAL SCHOLAR

A memory of Sir Harold Bailey,
sometime Professor of Sanskrit at Cambridge

The walls are covered with worn and faded books,
and books and papers are stacked untidily about the floor,
    some in cardboard boxes.

It is dark in the room, but a golden light
hangs low above the bended head and the old desk,
where, sharp as a sword, the master's pen
moves swiftly over waiting sheets.

In the silence, the signatures of a familiar script
    pass before him.

Here are words which will be set in place
upon long strings of kindred words,
even as the stones of a necklace are set together
in the company of other stones.

Here are voices which will sing again
the hymns and epics of far lands,
intone the sacred writings of the Avesta,
relive the peace and patience of the Buddha.

At the window a moth dusts the night air
    with restless wings.

OUT OF THE SILENCE

A Sonnet

See how he wanders careless through the world,
    This lithe and lonely reindeer from far lands!
What close and crafted art is here unfurled,
    The noble features etched by unknown hands.
The long, straight head, in browsing, is bent low,
    And fading pigments still old hues portray, –
The neck and shoulders white as recent snow,
    The hair behind flecked lightly brown or grey.

And how correctly are the legs defined:
Each waits, so well observed, in its true place
To take the next step forward. With slow grace
He moves through grasses swaying in the wind.
So may we tell our scene. It was first drawn
Within the silent caves of Stone Age man.

A HISTORY OF LETTERS

'Words are the instruments of our thoughts'

Strange pictographs were drawn in times bygone,
And pressed with reed-pens on the yielding clay –
Long-silent syllables that in their day
Declared the thoughts of distant Babylon
Whereby her hopes and fears again we may portray.

Papyrus sheets from plants which graced the Nile
Bore ancient Egypt's words; far Asia
Etched early forms on bone; and India
Worked square, stone seals which keep their secrets
  still.
Distinctive were the scripts and writing media.

But soon these primal writings were outgrown
As fair, young alphabets assumed their place.
Man learned to spell, and shortly would embrace
A knowledge of the world that lay unknown
Before the world of books filled every working space.

Today relentless, free, the written word
Moves on. Through channel'd Earth her journeys wend
Or high above on pathways of the wind.
Mysterious are her ways, her sounds unheard;
All pales at last before the mystery of 'mind'.

LIFE-ENERGY

A while ago, a friend brought a plant to me.
It was a plumbago, as I would learn,
so named from its leaden sprays
of graceful, blue-grey flowers.
But this plant had no flowers. It was dying.

I took it to a nursery, and there a lady
who was wise and learned in the manners
of plants, pruned it carefully,
and set it in a large pot with fresh,
keen earth. I took it home, put it
in a warm place, and watered it lovingly
every day, for many days.

There came signs of stirring within the plant.
The dead leaves curled away, new leaves and
brave, young buds explored the long stalks,
until, with a great releasing
of energy and pent life, the plant burst
brilliantly into bloom like a supernova.

Yet more was I to learn; for, as I looked
upon it, I seemed to understand
that energy and life are one,
so that life as life-force, life-energy,
will have existed since the first Great Breath
of things, so to remain, until,
at Time's fading, the pale, blue-grey petals
of Creation fall silently to earth.

THE LIVING UNIVERSE

Down the high corridors of star-swift time,
A flying lens with fearless, eagle eyes
Pierces the deep, deep, deep, dark solitudes
Of space. It sees young, shy-brave galaxies
Far, far away and faint, so faint and far
A billion arcs of time have spun through night
Before their waves of light can wash at last
The shores of this poor Earth. Here are fierce words
Which could strike fear into uncertain minds,
Portraying space as cheerless, hostile, cold,
And far removed from our day's relevance.

But there is yet one soaring argument
Which may bring fresh perspective to our thought.
Could we but sense that energy and life
Are singular and one, not separate
Or of their kind distinct, then should we know
That every world abounds and spills with *life*
Since *energy* is fully everywhere.
The matter is not just a twist of words;
For let me take you to some lonely hill
Upon a night when our close eiderdown
Of clouds has slipped away, when all is still
And shining stars are silver in the sky.
Now let our wonder lift the veil of sight:
Behold! oh, see! the living Universe!

CHAUCERAMA

'Pilgrimes were they alle,
That toward Caunterbury wolden ryde.'

So, on that day, on that fair-dawning day,
They bridled horse and rode forth on their way.
They rode forth with their landlord from the inn
To pray and to pay homage at the shrine
Where, now at peace, the brave St. Thomas lay.

They rode forth from the inn that April day
And told brave tales of heroes on the way.
So rode the knight, monk, Madame Eglentine,
The prioress, and all, unto that shrine
Where, peacefully, the brave St. Thomas lay.

They rode, as they will ride, upon their way.
For, lost in time, their gentilesse will stay
Within our hearts and care, there to remain.
Forever will they ride to that far shrine
And to the brave St. Thomas homage pay.

TOODLE-OO

Lines written after a poem
by Robert Burns

I've tried tae cheer my readers dear
    wi' verses lang or short, O,
Wi' tales an' dissertations, – aye,
    an' poems of a sort, O.
The pantomime we went tae see,
    we rode the punts wi' Tom, O;
Tho', faith! the stories o' them baith
    wad mak a CD rom, O!

But o' my cares and hame affairs
    I've blether'd lang enough, O,
An' did I care tae tell thee mair
    I'd soon run oot o' puff, O.
Sae end my lays an' roundelays
    save for the ane or twa, O;
Then, reader dear, I do much fear
    'tis 'Fare thee well' for ay, O.

TRUTH CLEANS THE WOUND:
LOVE HEALS IT

Truth and his sword, a symbol in all lands,
The wide world knows; and one whose calming hands
The balm of kindness hold, whose lips are peace,
The world strives hard to know. Disputes might cease
If Truth *and* Love would govern our affairs, –
Not only one, but both in careful shares,
Proportionately. Alas! there lies our plight:
He would be wise who gets the mixtures right.

THE LITTLE THINGS

One day when saddened by the stress and strife
 That sorely bleeds the world, and I had said:
'What can one do to ease the pains of life?'
 This shining thought strayed tip-toe through my head:
  Heaven is grateful for little things.

The life-protecting prayer, the happy song,
 The smile that bids the flowers of Spring awake;
The gentle word that seeks to right a wrong
 Based on the last, best judgment one can make:
  Heaven is grateful for little things.

The humble gift, the tiny sacrifice,
 The simplest act of courage and strong will;
For sweet forgiveness with her childlike face –
 There never was a wound she could not heal:
  Heaven is grateful for little things.

One need not be a saint to play some part:
 No need to slay a dragon every day.
Compassion's loving care, a beating heart,
 The arm that helps the lame one on his way:
  Heaven is grateful for little things.

THE END OF ACT ONE

An imaginative reconstruction

It is the finale of the First Act of the Play.

The engines of mass destruction are silent;
It is not a time of war.

Yet the silence is not the silence of peace,
and searching minds are not at ease.

The stage is dark. A roll of drums,
    growing ever louder,
tells that the Earth is in travail.
Men in their alarm cry,
    "What is ailing her?"[1]

There is a great crumbling.
It is the time of the final breaking down
    of wrong patterns of wealth,
of the golden altars of the anti-Christ.

There is a sound of trumpets,
    and a great light.

---

[1] From The *Qur'an*, Sura XCIX, verse 3.